THE HOLY ROMAN EMPIRE

Power Politics and the Papacy

by Anne Davison

Copyright©2014 Anne Davison

Books for Busy People

TABLE OF CONTENTS

MAPS

Page

PREFACE

This is the third book in the *'In Brief' Series: Books for Busy People,* the others being *From the Medes to the Mullahs; a History of Iran* and *Paul of Tarsus; a First Century Radical.* As with the previous books, the content of this book began as a series of lectures. They are aimed at the general reader who wants to understand a particular historical topic but doesn't have the time or inclination to read a heavy academic tome.

This book traces the history of the Holy Roman Empire, which lasted for over a thousand years, from the reign of Charlemagne in AD 800 until AD 1806 when it was dissolved following defeat by Napoleon. It is an Empire that had no fixed boundaries and until the 16th century, when the Habsburgs settled in Vienna, it had no permanent imperial city. At different periods its territories stretched from the North Sea to the Balkans and for a time in the 16th century included the South Americas.

The first chapter covers the rise of the Carolingian Empire in the 9th century and then its subsequent division into regions that roughly equate to modern France and Germany. Chapter Two looks at the period of the Ottonian dynasty, a time when many of the structures of the Imperial Church were put in place. The third chapter covers the Salian dynasty and conflict with the Papacy over the issue of Lay Investiture.

Chapter Four covers the role of the Prince Electors and the process for the election of the Emperor. The last two chapters are devoted to the Habsburgs, a dynasty that lasted from the 12th century until modern times and includes the dissolution of the Holy Roman Empire, the foundation of the Austrian Empire and finally the fall of the Austria-Hungarian Empire after World War I.

INTRODUCTION

Francois-Marie Arouet, better known as Voltaire, famously said that 'the Holy Roman Empire was neither Holy, nor Roman nor an Empire'. Taken at face value this is probably right. If we dig a little deeper, however, we may discover how and why, this entity came to be so named.

The foundation of the Holy Roman Empire is traditionally dated from the coronation of Otto the Great in AD 962. However, the reign of Charles I, otherwise known as 'the Great' or Charlemagne, who was crowned Emperor of the Romans by Pope Leo III on Christmas Day AD 800, is usually considered to be the first Emperor of the Empire.

The coronation of Charles was a key event in European history because it marked the revival of empire in Western Europe following the fall of the Western Roman Empire in the 5th century AD. Charles the Great was seen as the direct successor to Caesar Augustus and the Carolingian Empire successor to the Ancient Roman Empire. As such, Charles, and each successive Emperor, expected to rule with the same power and authority as had the Emperors of ancient Rome. This relationship with ancient Rome was central to the self-understanding of all Emperors from Charlemagne to Francis II in the 19th century and it also affected the on-going relationship between the Emperor and the Pope.

When Charles I was crowned in AD 800, the Pope anointed him as both Defender and Propagator of the Christian Faith. Crucially he was being crowned Emperor of a Christian Empire, otherwise known as Christendom. Following the European Reformation in the 16th century, all later Emperors, down to Francis II, who capitulated to Napoleon in AD 1806, viewed themselves as Defenders of the Roman Catholic Church and the Papacy.

The Holy Roman Empire is difficult to define; it was not an empire in the territorial sense, but was more a confederation of kingdoms and principalities of all sizes; from a single castle with its estates, to a vast kingdom. It lasted almost a thousand years from AD 962 until AD 1806 but had no capital city or clear boundaries. Its influence spread across most of Europe and for a short time under Charles V in the 16th century parts of South America also came under its sovereignty.

In theory the emperors were elected, but very often the title was passed on to a son thereby establishing dynasties, for example the House of Hohenstaufen between the 11th and 13th centuries and the later Habsburgs who ruled almost continuously from the middle of the 15th century onwards.

The early emperors chose their own capital: for Charles the Great it was Aachen, Otto the Great it was Magdeburg, Otto III it was Bamberg. The later Habsburgs settled in Vienna.

For much of its history the power lay not with the Emperor but with the great nobles and magnates of central Europe who made up the Electoral College. It was an Empire riddled with complex politics and the relationship between the Emperor and the Papacy was extremely volatile, ranging from an intense suspicion to open hostility.

CHAPTER ONE

The Carolingians

Fall of the Ancient Roman Empire

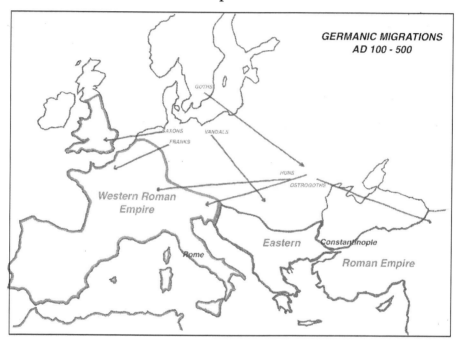

When the Roman Emperor Constantine the Great became a Christian in AD 313 he promulgated an edict, known as the Edict of Milan, which gave Christians freedom of worship in the Roman Empire for the first time. In AD 380, under Emperor Theodosius, the Edict of Thessalonica was issued ordering all subjects of the Roman Empire to profess the Christian faith, so making Christianity the state religion of the Empire. As Emperor, Constantine assumed responsibility for the spiritual wellbeing of all his subjects, while matters of doctrine were to be the responsibility of the bishops. However, it was to be the task of the Emperor to ensure that heresy was rooted out and that the Church remained united.

From the very beginning the relationship between Emperor and Church was potentially open to conflict. From the time of Theodosius in the 4th century there have been numerous cases where the Emperor and Patriarch in the East, or Emperor and Pope in the West, have clashed over questions of authority.

By the beginning of the 5th century the stability of the Empire was not threatened by religious tension from within, but by an outside threat from the North. Ever since the 2nd century there had been a gradual movement of tribal peoples across the Rhine and Danube, rivers that marked the Northern boundary of the Empire. Historically these migrations have been referred to as the Barbarian Invasions but today they are more correctly termed the Germanic Migrations, which reflects the fact that these people were seeking a better life, perhaps due to climatic change or fleeing oppression from invading tribes, rather than crossing the Rhine or Danube as aggressive invaders.

The tribes came from the Baltic region and Central and Northeast Asia. Saxons and Franks migrated from North-Western Europe into Britain and France; Goths and Vandals migrated into Central Europe and Huns migrated from the North-East into Central Europe. Another group, the Visigoths, migrated as far South as Spain where they established a sophisticated Christian kingdom.

By AD 450 these Germanic peoples had settled and integrated into the Western part of the Roman Empire to such an extent that the foundation of the Empire was beginning to weaken. In AD 476 a Germanic soldier named Odoacer deposed the Western Roman Emperor Romulus Augustus and became King of Italy. This traditionally marks the end of the Roman Empire in the West and the beginning of what is sometimes referred to as the 'dark ages'. The Roman Empire in the East, known as Byzantium, survived for almost another thousand years.

Islamic Threat from the South

During the so-called 'Dark Ages' that followed the fall of the Western Roman Empire another power, Islam, spread from its roots in Saudi Arabia Eastwards across Mesopotamia into modern Iraq and Iran, and Westwards along the coast of North Africa. In AD 711 a Muslim General named *Tariq ibn Ziyad* landed with his troops on what is now known as the Rock of Gibraltar, thereafter named the 'Mountain of Tariq' - *Jabal Tariq* in Arabic - from which the name Gibraltar is derived.

Later in the same year the Muslim armies defeated the defending Visigoths who were then the Christian rulers of Spain, at the Battle of Guadalete. By AD 717 the Muslims had crossed the Pyrenees into France but were finally checked in AD 732 at the famous Battle of Tours (Poitiers) by Charles Martel. It was Martel who was credited with having saved Christian Europe, indeed Western civilisation, from Islam. Charles Martel was the grandfather of Charles the Great, known as Charlemagne, the first Emperor of the Holy Roman Empire.

Charles the Great

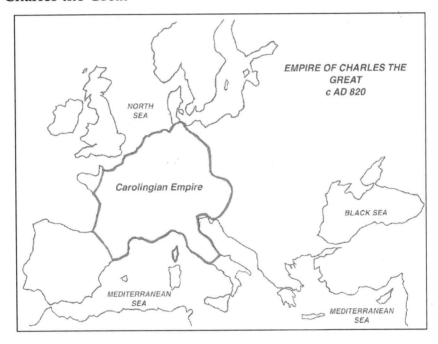

When Charles Martel died in AD 752, his son Pepin, known as the Short succeeded as the first Carolingian King. He was extremely devout, having been educated by the monks of St. Denis and throughout his rule he was a strong supporter of the Papacy against the Lombards in Northern Italy. In the process of overcoming the Lombards he secured several Italian cities on behalf of the Papacy and these later formed the Papal States. Together with his younger brother, Pepin also succeeded in subduing other tribes including the Bavarians, Aquitanians, Saxons and the Alemannia.

In AD 768 Charlemagne succeeded his father as King of the Franks. Little is known about his early life but he was probably born around AD 742, ten years after the Battle of Tours. He continued his father's campaign against the Saxons and by AD 785 he had, with some force, converted all the Saxon tribes to Christianity and imposed a strict Frankish administration upon them. At the head of an extremely strong army he also campaigned in the North-East against the Slavs, so bringing vast territories of the North-East into the Carolingian orbit.

Charlemagne continued his father's policy as Defender of the Papacy against the Lombards and in recognition of this, in AD 774, he was crowned King of the Lombards. Above all, Charlemagne was recognised as the great champion and protector of Christendom against all its enemies; pagans, heretics, the Byzantines and the Muslims.

On Christmas Day in the year AD 800, during Mass at St Peter's in Rome, Pope Leo III crowned Charles Emperor and Augustus of the Romans. Although there has been some debate as to whether or not Charlemagne was taken by surprise by the Pope's action, it is generally thought that he had been prepared. For example, he had surprisingly dressed in Roman style, rather than his more usual Frankish clothing.

As with his Roman predecessor Constantine, Charlemagne subsequently saw himself as the One Emperor ruling One Empire united under One Church and One Christianity.

He immediately began to organise the imperial Church by dividing it into twenty- one bishoprics, with Rome taking precedence. He called Church Councils and he took upon himself the responsibility for devising a new liturgy appropriate for the Western Church as opposed to that of the Eastern Byzantines. For example, it was under Charlemagne that the Western Church inserted the *filioque* (and the Son) clause into the Nicene Creed, which was contrary to what had been agreed at the First Ecumenical Council in AD 324 under Constantine. This was later to be one of the contributing factors to the schism between the Eastern and Western churches in AD 1054.

Charlemagne also supported the foundation of numerous monasteries and made the Church responsible for the education and spiritual wellbeing of the people. The structures put in place by the Carolingian Church in the early 9th century remained largely untouched until the time of Napoleon in AD 1806.

The coronation of Charles as Emperor of the Romans by the Pope understandably caused some consternation in the Eastern Roman Empire, which considered itself the only legitimate heir of Ancient Rome. In order to address this problem there were attempts to unite the Carolingians with the Byzantines through political marriages. While this did not work in the 9th century, it was a practice that became increasingly common in later centuries, particularly under the Habsburgs.

Charles himself had five wives in succession and numerous concubines. His marriages were largely political, aimed at uniting various parts of his Empire. For example, he married a Frank, a Lombard, a Swabian, an East Frank and finally another Swabian.

He chose Aachen as his capital where his famous throne still draws pilgrims and tourists to this day.

The Treaty of Verdun

As was normal practice with the earlier Merovingians and the Carolingians, surviving sons jointly inherited property and land on the death of a king, resulting in the kingdom or empire being weakened by constant division. This often led to brothers competing among themselves for territory, even to the point of waging war against each other.

When Charlemagne died in AD 814 his only surviving son, Louis I, known as the Pious, became sole ruler of the Empire. However, when Louis died in AD 840, he was survived by three sons; Lothair I, Louis the German and Charles the Bald. As the eldest, Lothair claimed over-lordship of the whole Empire, an act that was challenged by both Louis and Charles. This resulted in a three year war known as the Carolingian Civil War. The conflict was finally settled with the Treaty of Verdun AD 843, the conditions of which divided the Empire of Charlemagne into three. Charles the Bald inherited West Francia, roughly equating to modern day France. Louis the German inherited East Francia, roughly modern Germany and Lothair inherited the Middle Kingdom, known as Lotharingia, which comprised the Low Countries, Lorraine, Alsace, Burgundy, Provence and the Kingdom of Italy. The Treaty of Verdun is extremely significant for European history because it marks the beginning of modern Germany and France. It is also interesting to note that Verdun is the location where, centuries later during the First World War, France and Germany were in conflict.

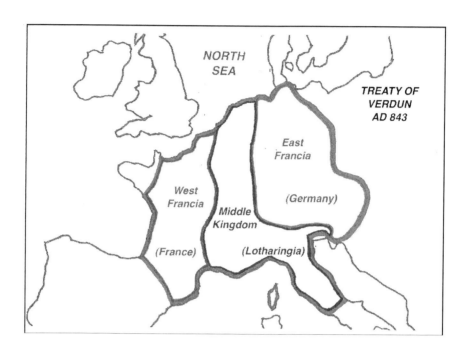

NORTH
SEA

TREATY OF
VERDUN
AD 843

East
Francia

West
Francia

Middle
Kingdom

(Germany)

(France)

(Lotharingia)

CHAPTER TWO
The Ottonian Empire

For approximately the next hundred years, following the Treaty of Verdun, the descendants of the Carolingians faced their greatest threat from the Danes, Slavs and Magyars of the North. In order to defend themselves, the main German tribes, comprising the Franks, Saxons, Swabians, Bavarians and Thuringians, jointly elected a leader as king. However, his role as king was only effective at a time of external threat. It was then his task to gather an army from all the tribes and as head of this army defend Christendom against the pagan threat. Once the threat was eliminated, his role as 'king over the tribes' ended and he returned to his previous status, having authority just over his own particular tribal kingdom. This set the pattern for the later Holy Roman Empire and is an illustration of the limited power that the King of the Romans, or Emperor had over the entire Empire.

In AD 936 the Franks and the Saxons chose Otto I, known as the Great, as their King. Following ratification by the remaining tribal duchies he was crowned King of the Germans at Aachen, the imperial city of Charles the Great. Otto, who was the illegitimate son of Henry I, was uneducated, but he proved to be a wise diplomat and a great military leader.

His first wife was Edgitha, sister of the English King Athelstan. As a wedding present Edgitha received the town of Magdeburg and it is here in Magdeburg Cathedral that she was buried with her husband. In AD 2008 some archaeologists working on the site discovered her tomb. Her remains were then taken to Bristol University where tests were carried out on the bones and teeth in order to ascertain whether or not she might be the sister of Athelstan. The scientists were able to confirm that the deceased had indeed spent her earlier years drinking water from Southern England. This seemed to be sufficient proof that the remains were those of Edgitha of England, in which case they are the oldest surviving remains of an English royal yet discovered. Her body was reinterred at Magdeburg Cathedral on 22nd October AD 2010.

The Battle of Lech

10th August AD 955 was a defining moment, not only in the life of Otto I, but also in the history of Germany, the Holy Roman Empire, indeed for Europe at large. For some time the Magyars, tribal people from Central Europe, and forerunners of the Hungarians, had been making incursions into German territory. Although many of the Magyars, including their leaders, were already Christian, having been baptised under the Eastern rite of Constantinople, the Germans still viewed them as pagan barbarians, monsters from the East and enemies of Christ.

When news arrived that the Magyars were moving Southwards again, this time in great hoards of possibly up to 10,000, Otto knew that his credibility as King of the Germans and Romans, and as Defender of Christendom, was at stake. He gathered together a combined army including Bavarians, Swabians, Franconians and Bohemians. Exact figures for both sides are uncertain except for the fact that the Magyars probably outnumbered Otto's troops.

Against all odds, Otto's army was successful in defeating the Magyars at the famous Battle of Lech, or Lechfield, which is close to Augsburg. The repercussions of this victory were profound.

In victory Otto was proclaimed Emperor. In February AD 962, at a service in Rome, Pope John XII crowned him Holy Roman Emperor. This was to be the official date for the founding of the Holy Roman Empire.

The Papacy at this time was extremely weak, largely because of corruption. Otto took advantage of this situation by assuming responsibility for appointing senior clerics and bishops, some of whom were his own relatives. This was the beginning of a period when the Emperor's power was greater than that of the Pope. He also founded bishoprics and cathedrals, giving that of Magdeburg an importance on a par with Rome.

The Battle of Lech marked the end of any further Magyar, or Hungarian, incursions into German territory and for a while the region continued to be contested between the Catholic Church in Rome and the Orthodox Church in Constantinople. However, by AD 972 Hungary was aligning itself with Rome and under King Stephen the country became a Western feudal state following the Catholic rite.

Otto I died in AD 973, by which time not only Hungary had been brought into the Holy Roman Empire, but also most of the Italian peninsula. His reign witnessed unprecedented church and cathedral building and under his patronage monastic foundations became centres of learning that produced many valuable illuminated manuscripts. The structures of the Imperial Church put in place by Otto the Great remained intact until modern times.

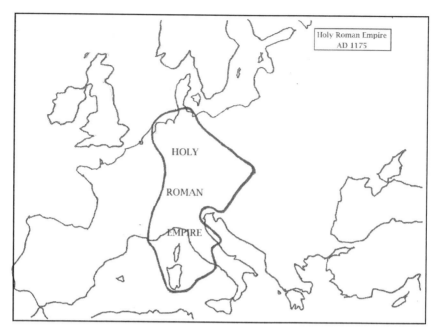

Otto I was succeeded by his son Otto II, who had already been King of Germany for twelve years and co-Emperor with his father for five. The Ottonian dynasty died out with Henry II in AD 1024. Henry, known as the Saint in recognition of his support of the Church, left no heir and so the crown then passed to Conrad II, a great-great-grandson of Emperor Otto I. Conrad was elected King of the Romans in AD 1024 and crowned Holy Roman Emperor in AD 1027, thus becoming the first monarch of the Salian dynasty, which ruled for a period of approximately 100 years.

CHAPTER THREE

The Salians and the Investiture Controversy

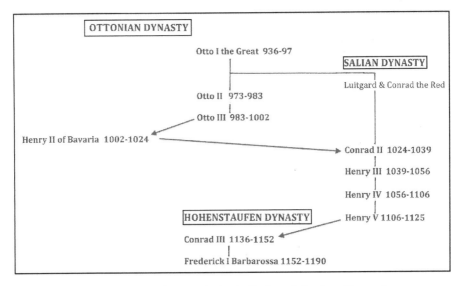

The Salians were Franks and their link with the Ottonians, who were Saxons, dated back to the marriage of Otto I's daughter Luitgard to the Salian Conrad the Red. Conrad II, the first Salian to become Holy Roman Emperor, was the great-great-grandson of Conrad the Red and Luitgard. This is an example, to be repeated throughout the history of the Holy Roman Empire, of the dynastic marriages that helped cement power within certain families.

The greatest event to mark the period of the Salians was a conflict between the Emperor and the Papacy, which is known as the Investiture Controversy. This led to some fifty years of German civil war and a great deal of power being taken away from the Emperor by the Papacy.

Throughout the period of the Ottonians and the early part of Salian rule, the Emperors believed they had been appointed by God with a divine right to rule all subjects of the Empire. Consequently it had been common practice for the Emperor to appoint bishops, abbots, and occasionally even Popes, many of whom were not even clerics, but lay members of his own family. They received lucrative positions and became wealthy landowners and feudal lords in their own right.

This practice of lay investiture not only undermined the power of the Papacy but it also encouraged corruption in the form of *simony*, whereby bishoprics and monastic houses were sold to the highest bidder rather than to the most able candidate.

By the middle of the 11th century things began to change in the form of a new breed of Pope. Whereas many earlier Popes had been extremely weak and often corrupt, now a wind of change came in the form of the monk Hildebrand, who became Pope Gregory VII, known later as Gregory the Great.

Said to come from humble origins, Hildebrand was at one time chaplain to Pope Gregory VI. He also spent some time at the famous Abbey of Cluny and finally rose to the position of Archdeacon. He spoke out against clerical abuse and corruption and became extremely popular both within the *curia* at the Vatican and with the people of Rome. He was unanimously elected Pope in AD 1073. However the election was irregular in that the Emperor had not been consulted, as was normal practice.

The Walk to Canossa

Gregory VII was determined to stop the practice of lay investiture. He believed that as God's spiritual representative on earth, only he had the right to appoint Bishops and Abbots. The issue came to a head in AD 1076 when the then Emperor, Henry IV, installed his own chaplain, a priest named Tedald, as Bishop of Milan despite the fact that the Pope had already named another, Atto, as candidate for the position. This was not the first time that Henry and the Pope had come into conflict and Gregory VII reacted to this latest outrage by excommunicating the Emperor and deposing him as King of Germany.

Initially Henry ignored the excommunication but some of his nobles took advantage of his reduced status, seized royal property and established independent fiefdoms of their own. Henry was quickly losing control; he finally gave in and decided to seek the Pope's forgiveness. In AD 1077 he travelled to Canossa in Northern Italy where the Pope was staying at the castle of Matilda of Tuscany, who was a great supporter of the Papacy. Despite it being midwinter, he stood barefoot, wearing only a hair shirt, for three days at the gate of the castle awaiting the Pope's forgiveness. This event has become known as *The Walk to Canossa*.

Gregory lifted the excommunication. However, the German nobles, who had benefitted from Henry's disgrace, were not prepared to give up the lands and property they had acquired. Furthermore, they even went on to elect a rival king, Rudolph von Rheinfeld.

Despite Henry's act of penitence he did not change his ways and in AD 1081 he proclaimed Clement III as anti Pope. He had Rudolph killed and then went on to attack Rome in order to remove Gregory and place Clement on the throne. In despair, Gregory called on the Normans of Southern Italy for help. The Normans agreed to come to the Pope's aid, but they were overzealous and in the process sacked the city of Rome creating outrage among the people. Consequently the angry citizens forced Gregory to leave the city and he later died in exile a sad and bitter man.

Henry's battle with the papacy continued throughout the brief reign of Pope Victor III and into that of Pope Urban II, who was a great supporter of Pope Gregory VII and his ecclesiastical reforms. Urban became Pope in AD 1088 but he was unable to take his seat in Rome because it was still occupied by the anti Pope Clement III, who had been placed on the throne by Emperor Henry IV.

Urban eventually succeeded in gaining universal recognition as Pope as a result of his successful preaching of the First Crusade at Clermont in AD 1095. Although the call to arms was officially in response to a request from the Byzantine Emperor *Alexios Komnenos* for help against the Seljuk Turks, it has been suggested that Urban seized this opportunity to unite the problematic warring factions of the West against a common foe; that of the Muslim Turks. The tactic worked and when he then added that the intention was also to liberate Jerusalem, Urban II succeeded in uniting armies from right across Western Europe under the banner of the cross.

The First Crusade was a Papal crusade. Since Henry IV and Urban II were enemies at the time the Emperor played no part in it, despite the fact that Henry had been crowned as Defender and Protector of Christendom against the heathen. The only Emperor of note to take part in the Crusades to the Holy Land was Frederick I, known as Frederick Barbarossa on account of his red hair, who actually died in Southern Anatolia in AD 1190 while taking part in the Third Crusade. The Third Crusade was also known as the Kings' Crusade because three European kings: Frederick Barbarossa of Germany, Philip Augustus of France and Richard the Lionheart of England, all took part.

The Concordat of Worms AD 1122

The issue regarding lay investiture and other reforms initially called for by Gregory VII, known as Gregorian Reforms, were finally settled at the Concordat of Worms in AD 1122. Both clerical celibacy and the outlawing of *simony*, the sale of church offices, became official canon law at this time.

But it was the decision regarding lay investiture that was to have the greatest impact on the power of the Emperor. It had always been Gregory VII's aim to free the Church from secular control and this was partially achieved at the Concordat of Worms. From AD 1122 the Emperor no longer had the right to select bishops and abbots; rather bishops would be elected by the canons of the cathedral and abbots by the monks of monasteries. Furthermore, only senior clerics had the right to invest a candidate with the sacred symbols of episcopal office: the ring and staff. However, the Emperor or his representative had the right to invest the candidate with the symbol of worldly power, the sceptre.

A further compromise allowed the Emperor or his representative to be present at the election process in order to resolve any possible disputes. Not surprisingly this meant that, over time, the Emperor was able to ensure that his favoured candidate got the job. These regulations only applied to Germany; Burgundy and Italy had different rules. England also had her own difficulties over lay investiture but the parties concerned only involved the Papacy and the English monarchy and not the Holy Roman Emperor.

The rules regarding the election of the Pope have varied over time. Initially the Pope was required to swear an oath of loyalty to the Holy Roman Emperor. In AD 1059 it was decreed that the cardinals should elect a candidate who would only take office after ratification by the clergy and laity. In AD 1139, not long after the Concordat of Worms, the need for the approval of the clergy and laity was removed, leaving the cardinals with exclusive right of election. This very much reflected the mood at a time when the power of the Papacy over the secular was in the ascendency.

The immediate effect of the Concordat of Worms in AD 1122 was to limit the power of the Emperor but the period of instability that preceded the Concordat did untold damage to the cultural life of Germany. At the beginning of the 11th century German monasteries led the way in theological and scholastic learning. This all came to an end during almost fifty years of civil war, when the intellectual life of Germany stagnated and fell behind other European countries. While universities were founded in Bologna, Paris, Oxford and Cambridge between the years AD 1088 and AD 1207, it was not until more than a hundred years later, in AD 1386 that the first German university was founded at Heidelberg.

CHAPTER FOUR

The Prince Electors

From the time of Otto I in the 10th century the emperors were, in theory, elected. This was considered preferable to an inherited monarchy, which resulted in too much power being held within one dynastic family. However, powerful dynasties did emerge, such as the Ottonians and Salians, as can be seen from previous chapters and will be seen later with perhaps the greatest of all dynasties, that of the Habsburgs.

Throughout the history of the Holy Roman Empire there existed a struggle for power between various factions, both clerical and lay. Apart from the continuing conflict between the Emperor and the Papacy as to who had supreme authority over the Empire, there had always existed a delicate balancing of power between the Emperor and his various vassals: princes, nobles and dukes. No party wanted another to become too powerful, even if that party was the Emperor himself. As was seen earlier, when the hapless Henry IV fell foul of Pope Urban II, his vassals quickly took advantage of the situation to build up their own fiefdoms by seizing the property of the Emperor at a time when he was unable to defend himself.

Under Charles the Great and the Carolingians the monarchy was hereditary, but this changed from the 10th century with the Ottonians. The principle of election dates back to the early centuries of the Germanic migrations. In those days it was usual practise for the various tribes to unite against a common foe and then to choose one of the most able as overall leader, or king, from one of the tribes. Such a leader only held power at time of war. Once peace was resumed the king's power reverted to his particular domain. When Otto I was unanimously proclaimed Emperor at the Battle of Lech he was already king of the Romans, but by proving his leadership skills on the battlefield he was proclaimed Emperor, a practice that mirrored that of Ancient Rome.

From the very beginning, any candidate for that of Emperor had first to be elected and crowned King of the Romans, a title that became synonymous with King of the Germans. Only then would he go to Rome in order to be crowned Emperor by the Pope. The title King of the Romans had nothing to do with the city of Rome; rather it reflected that he was King of the Roman people who were scattered across the Empire. Once more this reflected the situation in Ancient Roman Empire.

It was quite normal for a ruling monarch to prepare and propose his own son or one of his other male relatives to be his successor. Rather than oppose the monarch's intention, an act that could have led to civil war, the leaders or rulers of the tribal fiefdoms usually acquiesced.

Initially, all the people could take part in the electoral process. First the most powerful nobles would select one candidate from a shortlist and this choice had to be unanimous. The minor nobility were then required to approve the choice of candidate and finally there followed the acclamation of the people. In this way all levels of society played a part. However, over time and largely for pragmatic reasons, the final stage, that of the approval of the minor nobility and the acclamation of the people, came to be taken for granted. Furthermore, the privilege of choosing the candidate was narrowed down to the rulers of the seven most powerful kingdoms or dukedoms. These seven became known as the Prince Electors.

The one serious fault with the system was that there was no means of arbitration, apart from war. This was more or less the situation that existed between the 10th and 14th centuries.

The Golden Bull of AD 1356

A particularly bloody conflict occurred in the early part of the 14th century between two rival kings: Louis IV and Frederick the Fair, both claiming to be the legitimately elected King of the Romans and therefore the legitimate Holy Roman Emperor. As a result, when Charles IV, King of Bohemia was later unanimously elected King of the Romans in AD 1346, he was determined to avoid any further possible conflict. In AD 1356 he promulgated a Golden Bull, a decree that put in place a clearly defined and legal, electoral process that was to remain in force for more than four hundred years until AD 1806, when the last Emperor abdicated following the invasion of Napoleon.

The most important aspect of the new legislation was the formalisation of the Electoral College. From this time on there were to be seven Electors made up of both ecclesiastic and secular leaders. The ecclesiastics included the Archbishops of Cologne, Mainz and Trier, being the oldest and richest sees. The secular Electors reflected something of the original tribes: the Duke of Saxony, (the Saxons) the Palatine of the Rhine (originally Bavarians), the Margrave of Brandenburg and the King of Bohemia. Strictly speaking Bohemia did not fit because it was not German, but since the King of Bohemia promulgated the Bull, then its inclusion should not surprise us. Although the number of Electors later varied, from the outset the number seven, having some sacred significance, was considered the ideal number.

In order to qualify for election a candidate had to be a man of good character and over 18 years. All four of his grandparents were expected to be of noble blood. No law required him to be a Catholic, though imperial law at that time assumed that he was and he did not need to be a German. Again, this latter point probably reflects the involvement of the King of Bohemia.

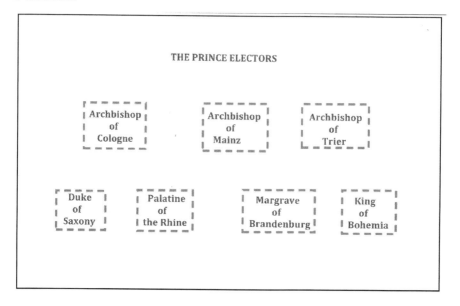

THE PRINCE ELECTORS

Archbishop of Cologne   Archbishop of Mainz   Archbishop of Trier

Duke of Saxony   Palatine of the Rhine   Margrave of Brandenburg   King of Bohemia

During the Thirty Years War, which raged across Europe between AD 1618 and AD 1648, the Duke of Bavaria was added to replace the Palatine of the Rhine, who had temporarily lost his title and vote. In AD 1692 a ninth Elector was added, that of the Duke of Brunswick-Luneburg who became Elector of Hanover. In AD 1714 the then Elector was George I, who also assumed the crown of Great Britain on the death of Queen Anne. This was because under the terms of the Acts of Union in AD 1707, only a Protestant could inherit the British throne and although there were many Catholics more closely related to Queen Anne, George, being a Lutheran was the closest eligible Protestant.

Other provisions of the Golden Bull of AD 1356 stipulated that Frankfurt, being on Frankish soil, should be the location of the election and the Archbishop of Mainz should be the convener. All coronations should take place at Aachen on the throne of Otto I and that Nuremburg should be the location of the first Diet. It should be said that none of this was revolutionary; the Bull merely regularised what had largely been the current practice.

The Reichstag

The Emperor had no autonomous power, other than the freedom to confer titles and to call Imperial Diets. Power had traditionally been in the hands of the nobility, which, by the 15th century formed the backbone of the Reichstag, which became the official legislative body, or assembly. The Emperor could, however, convene the Reichstag at any time and at any location. After the 17th century the Reichstag became a permanent body and consisted of three main Councils: the Council of the Prince Electors, mentioned above; the Council of Princes which included a secular branch and an ecclesiastic branch made up of Prince Bishops, Abbots and the Grand Masters of the Teutonic Knights and the Knights of St John and finally the Council of the Imperial Free Cities. These were cities under the direct sovereignty of the Emperor rather than local magnates and they enjoyed special privileges and tax exemptions.

Perhaps the best way to view the status of the Emperor is to see his role as a symbolic head of a federation of many kingdoms, principalities and dukedoms of various sizes. He had no power to intervene in the affairs of the individual kingdoms. He had no standing Imperial army and so at times of external threat he had to depend upon his vassal states to provide manpower. Furthermore, because he usually had to bribe the Electors in order to secure his election, with gifts of money or property, he became poorer as they became wealthier and their position became stronger as his weakened.

CHAPTER FIVE

The Habsburgs

The Habsburgs take their name from Habichtsburg Castle near Aargau in today's Switzerland. The acknowledged founder of the Habsburg dynasty, which lasted for some 600 years or more, is Rudolph, who reigned from AD 1273 to AD 1291. Rudolph was a godson of the Hohenstaufen Emperor Frederick II and he was on good terms with Frederick's son Conrad IV, King of the Germans, from whom he received generous grants of land.

During the chaos that followed the fall of the Hohenstaufen dynasty Rudolph was able to secure even more territory as well as purchase lands from feuding bishops and abbots. In this way he became one of the most powerful nobles of the time and in AD 1273 he was crowned King of the Romans in Aachen Cathedral. In AD 1276 he became ruler of Austria so marking the beginning of continuous Hapsburg rule in Austria until AD 1918.

Through a process of fortuitous dynastic marriages the Habsburg dominions came to include Spain, Burgundy, the Netherlands and for a short time in the 16th century under Charles V, the Americas. The Habsburgs also witnessed the traumatic upheaval of the Reformation and the resulting Thirty Years War, plus the constant fear of Turkish invasion from the East and intermittent conflict with France.

Maximilian I

The Habsburgs gained territory through diplomacy and political marriage rather than through war. They were obsessed with their lineage and, like so many other Holy Roman Emperors, saw themselves as direct descendants of Charles the Great.

From a long line of Habsburg Emperors, perhaps two stand out as being of particular interest: Maximilian I, (AD 1459 - AD 1519) and Charles V, (AD 1500 - AD 1558). Maximilian was a colourful, larger than life and popular ruler who, through a number of opportunistic dynastic marriages considerably extended Habsburg territory. Charles, his grandson, was a cold, complex yet competent character, who had the task of steering the Empire through perhaps one of the most difficult periods of European history.

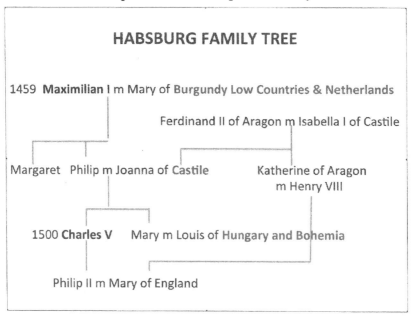

Maximilian was born in AD 1459. His father, Frederick III, who was the hereditary Duke of Austria, was the first Habsburg to be crowned Emperor. At the age of 37 Frederick married the daughter of the King of Portugal, a marriage which brought with it sufficient dowry to pay off his many debts.

It is said that Maximilian's childhood was far from ideal. In AD 1453, when he was only six years old, the Ottomans had captured Constantinople and the child regularly heard gruesome tales of the barbarity of the Turks from Hungarian and Croatian refugees.

Great expectations were placed on Maximilian. From early on in his life it was hoped that he would be the new Constantine who would save Christendom from Islam, just as the 4th century Constantine had promoted Christianity over the paganism of the Ancient Roman Empire. In recognition of this, Maximilian's mother changed her name to Helena in memory of Helena, the mother of Constantine the Great. It was even suggested that Maximilian himself might be called Constantine but this was too much for his father.

Maximilian lived life to the full. As a child he learned to paint and draw and he loved to be with 'ordinary' people: the sweepers, porters and tradespeople. As a young man he enjoyed carpentry, music, gastronomy, mining, shooting and the crossbow. He loved to hunt and to fish. It was said that he had an engaging manner and enjoyed dancing with the wives of Nuremburg, chatting with his mercenaries and his servants; indeed anyone he met.

He claimed to be able to speak seven languages but this has been questioned. He undoubtedly had an enquiring mind. He was an avid reader, enjoyed writing and philosophical debate and throughout his adult life he was a patron of the arts. He also commissioned many works from Albrecht Durer, the famous woodcut artist whose surviving works today give us an insight into the life and times of the Emperor.

One of the most significant events of Maximilian's reign was his fortuitous marriage to Mary, the daughter of Charles the Bold of Burgundy. Such a marriage brought benefits to both parties. It raised the status of Burgundy, which although rich and sophisticated, was nevertheless just a Dukedom, to that of a Kingdom. At the same time it brought Burgundy, the Low Countries and the Netherlands into the Holy Roman Empire of the Habsburgs.

Once the marriage was agreed, the couple began to study each other's portraits, as was usual for the time. By the 15th century court painters were beginning to paint portraits that reflected the individuality and personality of the subject and so we do have an idea of what Maximilian looked like. He was said to be good looking. He had his father's shoulder length reddish hair and long nose. Both were large men, but whereas Frederick was on the fat side, Maximilian was lean and muscular.

Frederick went to a great deal of expense, and thereby into debt, in order to make sure that his son was suitably escorted on his journey to meet is future bride. When they finally met in Ghent on the 20th May AD 1477, it was said to be love at first sight. Maximilian was then 18 and Mary was 20. They were married the next day.

Maximilian learned French from his wife and they both enjoyed hunting, hawking and above all skating. Sadly, in AD 1482, while on a hawking expedition, Mary fell from her horse and died. She was 25 years old. In AD 1493, eleven years later, Maximilian married Bianca, daughter of the Duke of Milan.

In AD 1486, just four years after the death of Mary, the 27 year old Archduke Maximilian was elected King of the Romans by the Electoral College. Apparently this did not please his father, who thought that his son was incapable of ruling the Empire. For seven years father and son ruled jointly and this proved to be a difficult time for Maximilian who was often treated more like a school boy than a co-ruler, being left to wait for hours before being granted an audience with his father.

When Frederick died at the age of 77 years following the amputation of a leg, the way was finally cleared for Maximilian to become Emperor. He immediately embarked upon an ambitious programme of reform; very often starting projects but never seeing them through. He was constantly on the move, perhaps staying at one of his many 'imperial palaces' for only a few days and in each of these residences he always had his writing desk.

Following in his father's footsteps Maximilian further extended Habsburg influence through dynastic marriages. The most significant and far-reaching was that of his only son Philip, known as the Handsome, to Joanna, daughter of Ferdinand and Isabella of Spain. Such a union brought Spain into the Habsburg orbit. Philip died young and his only other child, Margaret, was childless despite two marriages.

Maximilian then turned his attention to his grandchildren. In AD 1515 he met with King Ladislaus II of Hungary and Bohemia and at the First Congress of Vienna it was agreed that Maximilian's granddaughter Mary should marry Louis, the son of Ladislaus and that Maximilian's grandson Ferdinand should marry Ann, sister of Ladislaus. These marriages eventually brought Hungary and Bohemia under the Habsburgs.

Maximilian died on the 19th January AD 1519, in Wels, Upper Austria. For the previous five years he had been carrying his coffin around with him; most of his entourage believing that it was a treasure chest or contained books.

Throughout his life he had been a champion of the arts and literature. He supported many of the great painters, sculptors and writers of the day and during his rule towns such as Nuremburg, Regensburg and Bamburg were at their height, attracting the most talented of the time. Sadly many of these towns were bombed during the Second World War.

Charles V

Since Maximilian had no surviving son, his grandson, Charles V was crowned Holy Roman Emperor in succession in AD 1519 at the age of 19. While outwardly the succession appeared to be hereditary, the formality of election still had to be observed and other contenders for the crown included Francis I of France and Henry VIII of England. As was normal, in order to secure the throne, a great deal of behind the scenes lobbying took place, together with financial and other incentives; in other words, bribery. Charles secured the vote but only after having run up huge debts with the Fugger bankers.

Charles was born on the 24th February AD 1500 at Ghent where Mary, his grandmother had died after falling off her horse. Charles's father, Philip the Handsome and son of Maximilian, died in AD 1506 when he was just six years old. His mother Joanna, daughter of Ferdinand and Isabella and known as 'the mad' on account of her mental instability, lived in seclusion in Spain. As a virtual orphan Charles was brought up by his aunt, Margaret of Austria.

As the eldest son of Philip the Handsome, Charles inherited the throne of Spain, which by that time included the Spanish colonies of South America.

Charles's maternal grandparents, Ferdinand and Isabella, had founded the Spanish Inquisition in AD 1478, which was originally set up to test the loyalty of *Conversos*, Jews who had converted to Catholicism. Eventually all Jews became suspect and were finally expelled from Spain by Ferdinand and Isabella in AD 1492. Charles V and his son Philip II were to live through some of the worst excesses of this cruel machine, which continued in different forms until relatively recent times. As staunch Catholics both Charles V and Philip II supported the Inquisition, which was later used against Protestants following the European Reformation.

Catherine of Aragon, daughter of Ferdinand and Isabella, was the first wife of Henry VIII and therefore Queen of England. Catherine's sister was Joanna the Mad, Charles' mother, which made Charles the nephew of Catherine.

This was to put him in a very difficult situation. When Henry VIII asked for the Pope's agreement to a divorce between himself and Catherine, she appealed to her nephew Charles for support. Even if Charles had wished to meet with the Pope on behalf of Catherine, events were taken out of his hands because of the so-called 'Sack of Rome' in May AD 1527. This occurred after Charles was unable to pay his troops. His imperial forces had just defeated an alliance of France, the Papacy and various Italian States and they expected their pay. When none was forthcoming, some 34,000 imperial troops mutinied, ran riot through the City of Rome, killing and plundering as they went. The Pope, Clement VII, was just able to escape through a secret tunnel to the *Castel Sant'Angelo*.

A month later peace was restored, but only after the Pope agreed to pay a large ransom in exchange for his life, as well as the cession of several Italian cities to the Holy Roman Empire. The Pope's ordeal at the hands of Charles' troops also ensured that he could not afford to upset the Emperor again by agreeing to the annulment of the marriage between Henry VIII and Catherine of Aragon. This finally contributed to the events leading up to the English Reformation.

The Ottomans

From his grandmother's side Charles had inherited the lands of Burgundy, a region contested over by France. This resulted in an extremely difficult relationship with France, a situation that plagued Charles throughout his reign and frequently led to war. Another consequence of this animosity was the alliance that Francis I of France made with the Ottoman Sultan Suleiman the Magnificent: an alliance that was deliberately formed in order to oppose the Holy Roman Empire of the Habsburgs. In order to counter-balance this alliance Charles opened up negotiations with the Persian Safavids, another Islamic dynasty which, being *Shi'a*, were known enemies of the Ottomans who were *Sunni*. Although relations between Charles and the Safavids were good, the distances involved between the two powers made the alliance unworkable.

It was during the reign of Charles V that the Ottomans, led by Suleiman the Magnificent, first reached Vienna in AD 1529. Having successfully defeated the Serbs at the Battle of Blackbird's Field, near Kosovo in AD 1389, the Bulgarians in AD 1396 and the Hungarians at the Battle of Mohacs in AD 1526, Vienna was in sight and next in line. It is estimated that between 120,000 and 300,000 Ottoman troops had begun the march across Europe but this number was greatly depleted, largely due to bad weather, by the time they reached the walls of Vienna in late September.

Surrender negotiations between the two sides failed and Suleiman's troops started to bombard the city walls. On the Austrian side, Archduke Ferdinand was supported by troops from his brother Charles. The siege was short-lived. Suleiman was running short of supplies, his men were sick and some were deserting. By the middle of October Suleiman's troops were in retreat and Vienna was saved. The event, however, sent shock waves right across Europe and the Turk became the most feared enemy of the West.

The Reformation

When Martin Luther pinned his Ninety Five Theses against the sale of indulgences on the door of All Saints Church, Wittenburg in AD 1517, Charles V was just 17 years old. Despite his youth he soon became involved in the unfolding events. As Holy Roman Emperor he understood his role, as did all his predecessors and successors, as Protector and Defender of the Church against pagans and heretics.

Initially, he hoped that the disturbances that followed Luther's action would calm down but the reverse occurred; with the aid of the printing press, Luther's teachings spread and his supporters, including some members of the nobility, grew. After several attempts at reconciliation between Luther and the Pope's emissaries failed, Charles decided to intervene himself. He therefore summoned an Imperial Diet to be held at Worms, which took place between 28th January and 25th May AD 1521. The Emperor himself presided over part of the proceedings and this is the context where traditionally Luther is said to have uttered the famous words 'Here I stand, I can do no other'. However these words have never been found in the transcripts. What is clear is that on 25th May AD 1521 Charles V signed an Imperial Decree declaring Luther a heretic.

Luther had been promised safe conduct to and from the hearing at Worms but the Elector of Saxony, a supporter of Luther, decided to 'kidnap' him and take him for safe keeping to his castle at Wartburg where he was to stay for a year. During this time Luther produced many of his most famous writings and translations of the Bible into the German language.

The fact that the Elector of Saxony had intervened in this way is significant. Known as Frederick the Wise, he was a senior Elector of the Empire. At the time of Charles' election he was himself nominated as a candidate for the imperial throne by Pope Leo X. Although a loyal Catholic he also spoke out about the need for reform and he was supportive of Luther and his teaching.

Frederick is an example of many German princes who eventually came to support the Protestant calls for reform. Conflict between the Papacy and Emperor on the one hand and the Protestant princes on the other, eventually led to the Thirty Years War which raged across Germany between AD 1618 and AD 1648, killing up to 40% of its population.

The war officially came to an end with the Peace of Westphalia in AD 1648, the terms of which gave each prince the right to determine the religion of his own particular state, whether Roman Catholicism, Lutheranism or Calvinism. Furthermore, Christians living as a minority in any state, for example a Roman Catholic living in a Lutheran state, were guaranteed the right to worship in their own tradition.

The Catholic Church's response to the outcome of the Protestant Reformation was the Counter-Reformation. Also known as the Catholic Revival, it was a movement that was formally put in place by Charles V in AD 1545 at the Council of Trent. The Council worked on four major themes: Church structures, religious orders, spiritual movements and political considerations. Two outcomes in particular worth mentioning are the foundation of the Jesuits with its emphasis on teaching and the flowering of the baroque style in art and architecture, the purpose of which was twofold: first to symbolise the triumph of the Catholic Church over its enemies and second as a means of educating the people, many of whom were illiterate. This is the time when the Church commissioned so much religious art, for example the works of the famous painter *Caravaggio*.

The Protestant Reformation opened up a chasm across Europe and split the Holy Roman Empire. National Churches were formed in the Protestant countries of Germany, Scandinavia, Scotland and England. In many German states the Emperor simply became the titular head for his Protestant subjects, while in the same state he remained Defender and Advocate of the Church for his Catholic subjects. The Holy Roman Empire had been created under Charles the Great in AD 800 when the Empire was coterminous with the One Church. That unity had now been lost and with it the Empire's power went into decline.

Charles V's reign had been long and eventful. At heart he was a Spaniard and felt much more comfortable in his Spanish and Burgundian territories than in Germany where he was not very popular, partly because he never managed to speak very good German. Throughout his life he suffered from epilepsy but towards the end he was plagued by gout and in AD 1556 he decided to abdicate and spend his final years in a secluded monastery in Spain.

Before he died Charles passed his Spanish territories, including the South American colonies, to his son Philip II, and the crown of the Holy Roman Empire to his younger brother Ferdinand. Habsburgs continued to rule in Spain until AD 1661 when Charles II of Spain died leaving no heir, an event that eventually led to the War of the Spanish Succession between AD 1701 and AD 1714.

The Battle of Vienna

The Ottomans' dream of taking Vienna did not die in AD 1529 when their first attempt failed. It was just a question of time and as they waited for the right moment they prepared for their next advance towards Habsburg lands by repairing roads and bridges and organising ammunition centres at strategic points across the Balkans.

They were eventually convinced that the time might be right when Protestants in Habsburg occupied Hungary openly rebelled against the brutal policies of Leopold I, who reigned as Holy Roman Emperor between AD 1658 and AD 1705. Leopold was a staunch supporter of the Counter Reformation and he made no secret of his desire to crush the Protestants. In the conflict between the Protestant forces of Hungary and the Habsburgs, Ottoman forces came in on the side of the Protestants.

During AD 1681 and AD 1682 Leopold's forces gradually moved further Eastwards into Ottoman territory and at this point the Grand Vizier Mara Mustafa Pasha was able to convince the Sultan, Mehmet IV, that they should respond to this invasion of their territory by attacking Vienna.

By July AD 1683 the Ottomans were once again at the walls of Vienna. An army estimated at between 90,000 to 300,000 men, including troops from the Ottoman vassal state of the Crimea, surrounded the walls while the inhabitants of the city worked on its defenses and awaited reinforcements. After a siege lasting two months, battle ensued on the 12th September between the Ottoman forces and a combined force of Poland-Lithuania and the Holy Roman Empire that included forces from Bavaria, Saxony, Franconia, Royal Hungary and Swabia. Under the leadership of the King of Poland, Jan III Sobieski, the allied forces were victorious and the Ottomans retreated.

AD 1683 marked a watershed in central European history. Never again did the Turks attempt an invasion beyond Belgrade and from this point on the Ottoman Empire went into steady decline. At the same time, as the Ottomans retreated from Vienna, the Habsburgs retook territory that had previously been under Ottoman rule. So began a tug of war between the Ottomans and the Habsburgs over the Balkans that was to continue until the 20th century.

CHAPTER SIX

End of Empire

By AD 1700 the balance of power in the region had shifted quite dramatically. The Ottoman Empire was in decline as the Habsburgs gradually pushed into Hungary and beyond. On the other hand, the Holy Roman Empire had been losing both territory and influence in the Western part of the Empire since the European Reformation of the 16th century.

By the end of the 17th century the balance of power in the region was also affected by the growing influence of Russia under the rule of Peter the Great and the later ambitions of Catherine the Great. But it was from France that the real threat to the peoples of Europe came.

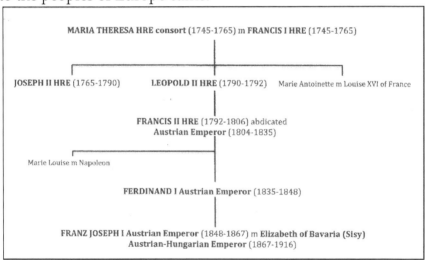

MARIA THERESA HRE consort (1745-1765) m FRANCIS I HRE (1745-1765)

JOSEPH II HRE (1765-1790)   LEOPOLD II HRE (1790-1792)   Marie Antoinette m Louise XVI of France

FRANCIS II HRE (1792-1806) abdicated
Austrian Emperor (1804-1835)

Marie Louise m Napoleon

FERDINAND I Austrian Emperor (1835-1848)

FRANZ JOSEPH I Austrian Emperor (1848-1867) m Elizabeth of Bavaria (Sisy)
Austrian-Hungarian Emperor (1867-1916)

Napoleon

The French Revolution in AD 1789 created ripples right across Europe, leaving monarchies fearful that the spirit of revolution would engulf their own subject peoples.

Perhaps the greatest symbol of this wind of change was the rise of a young Corsican military officer, Napoleon Bonaparte. Napoleon declared himself Emperor in AD 1804 of a new French Empire. He saw himself as another Charlemagne and his greatest ambition was to extend his empire to a point comparable with that of Charles the Great's Carolingian Empire of the 9th century, which stretched as far as Hungary and Moravia in the East. Relations between the Holy Roman Empire and France had never been good; now France posed a serious threat.

The Emperor at this time was Francis II, the eldest son of Leopold II. Francis spent the first few years of his life in Tuscany where his father was Grand Duke. However, knowing that he might one day become Emperor he was sent to the Imperial court in Vienna to be educated under the watchful and stern eye of his Uncle, Emperor Joseph II, who had no heir of his own. Francis then joined the army, serving with a regiment in Hungary and he adapted quickly into this disciplined style of military life.

Throughout his life Francis was acutely aware of the French threat. His own aunt, Marie Antoinette, had been executed along with her husband, King Louis XVI, in AD 1793 and he watched anxiously as German and Austrian lands were gradually being absorbed into Napoleon's Empire.

The catalyst came in December AD 1805, when Napoleon led his 'Grand Army' of some 200,000 men against an allied army comprising the Holy Roman Empire and the Russian Empire. The battle that ensued on the 2nd December AD 1805 is sometimes called 'The Battle of the Three Emperors', the Emperors being: Napoleon, Francis II and Tsar Alexander I of Russia. The battle is more commonly known as 'the Battle of Austerlitz'.

The outcome was a resounding victory for Napoleon, which resulted in the retreat of the Russian forces, but more significantly for Europe it marked the end of the Holy Roman Empire. On the 6th August AD 1806 Francis abdicated and dissolved the Empire. As so often happens in history, a marriage of convenience followed, with Francis' daughter, Marie Louis, marrying Napoleon and becoming Empress of France.

The Austrian Empire

Francis had been preparing himself for this eventuality for some time. In true Habsburg fashion he could never contemplate the end of the Imperial dynasty of the Habsburgs and so in AD 1804 he founded the Austrian Empire with himself entitled Francis I, Emperor of Austria.

In AD 1806, under the protectorate of Napoleon, some of the German princes formed the Confederation of Rhine States, which lasted until AD 1813. The Confederation effectively acted as a buffer region between France and Russia. Initially 16 German states were part of this new confederation and within two years another 19 had joined. In this way Napoleon had added large parts of German territory to his French Empire but neither Austria nor Prussia were members.

In AD 1813 Napoleon fought another battle against coalition forces at Dresden and once more he was victorious. However, later the same year he was confronted by a coalition army twice that of his own. It included Prussia, Austria, Sweden, Russia, Great Britain, Spain, and Portugal. This was the famous Battle of Leipzig, the largest battle of the Napoleonic wars. On this occasion Napoleon was defeated at a cost of over 90,000 casualties on both sides. The Battle of Leipzig also marked the end of the Confederation of the Rhine and the German States were now faced with looking towards a new future.

German Revolution and Nationalism

In AD 1814, after the fall of Napoleon and collapse of the Confederation of the Rhine, a Congress was called in Vienna. The aim was to decide the future of the states of the old Holy Roman Empire. One decision was to form the German Confederation, which was a loose league of 39 sovereign states, with the Austrian Emperor, Francis I, as President. Not surprisingly there were differences of opinion across the states, largely between the *Restorationists*, those who were traditionalists and wanted to retain the old monarchies, and the *Liberals* who were looking for more equality, improved working conditions but even more importantly, the possible unification of the German speaking people under a united Germany.

The *Restorationists* came together as a 'Concert of Europe', which included Austria, Prussia, Russia and the United Kingdom; all were monarchies and fearful of revolution on their own doorsteps. A leading figure of the group was Prince Clemens von Metternich who was Foreign Minister of the Austrian Empire and instrumental in bringing about the marriage between Marie Louis and Napoleon. He was also known to take repressive action against the liberals of the German Confederation and this finally led, in AD 1848, to both the German Revolution and the demise of the Concert of Europe.

By the middle of the 19th century nationalism and calls for national unification were commonplace. Greece freed herself from the Ottoman Empire and became an independent country in AD 1821 and Italy, which had begun the process in AD 1815, was finally unified in AD 1861.

AD 1871 marked both the unification of Germany and the beginning of the German Empire. Key to this was the defeat of the French by the Prussians in the Franco-Prussian War of AD 1870-71. Prussia by that time was the largest and most powerful of the German states with Otto von Bismarck as Minister President of the Kingdom of Prussia. It was Bismarck who masterminded the Unification of Germany. Becoming the first Chancellor he was also instrumental in the creation of the German Empire, which included most of the Germanic speaking areas apart from Austria. It could be argued that Germany felt the need to have its own empire in order to counter balance the Austrians, which, in AD 1867 had been formed into the Austria-Hungarian Empire, or dual monarchy of Austria and Hungary. The first Emperor of the new German Empire was William I of the House of Hohenzollern.

Austria-Hungarian Empire

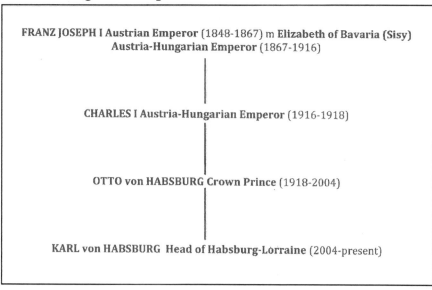

FRANZ JOSEPH I Austrian Emperor (1848-1867) m Elizabeth of Bavaria (Sisy)
Austria-Hungarian Emperor (1867-1916)

CHARLES I Austria-Hungarian Emperor (1916-1918)

OTTO von HABSBURG Crown Prince (1918-2004)

KARL von HABSBURG Head of Habsburg-Lorraine (2004-present)

Ever since the Habsburgs had defeated the Ottomans in AD 1863, they had slowly been making inroads across the Balkans into areas that were traditionally either Orthodox Christian or Muslim. Many of these people, who had lived under Ottoman rule for centuries, were not happy finding themselves under the rule of what they saw as an oppressive and autocratic Roman Catholic Empire.

Even Hungary, which was a Roman Catholic country, and had not been occupied by the Ottomans to the same extent, were dissatisfied with Habsburg rule, largely because they felt they were treated as inferior to the Austrians. For much of its history, although functioning with a certain amount of automomy, part of Hungary had been officially under the rule first of the Ottomans and later the Habsburgs of Austria. In time the Hungarians came to resent this situation and pushed for total independence.

In response to a growing discontent, a compromise, known as 'The Compromise', was reached in AD 1867 with the formation of the dual monarchy of Austria and Hungary, otherwise known as the Austria-Hungarian Empire. Under this Compromise it was agreed that there should be a 'union of crowns'. In other words there should be one ruler over two independent and equal countries.   This arrangement was formalised with the coronation in Buda of Emperor Franz Joseph and Empress Elizabeth of Bavaria, also known as Sisy, as King and Queen of Austria. Franz Joseph and Elizabeth remained as Emperor and Empress of Austria as well as being King and Queen of Hungary; hence the 'Dual Monarchy'.

This is the Sisy who we see so often on chocolate boxes and is frequently compared to Princess Diana. When she and Franz Jospeh were first married they were seen as the perfect couple. He was slim and handsome and as with so many of his predecessors, he had spent time in the army and was usually portrayed in a smart military uniform. She was stunning; very slim with beautiful eyes and waist length brown hair. But the marriage was not successful and Empress Elizabeth gradually came to spend more time away from court than by her husband's side. There has been much speculation about their marriage but whatever the truth, the Empress clearly was happier visiting other European countries, including England, where she spent much of her time hunting and riding.

Elizabeth's unhappy life came to a violent end in AD 1898 when, whilst visiting Geneva she was stabbed to death with a pair of scissors by an anarchist. The other tragedy within the family was the death of her eldest son, Crown Prince Rudolph. In AD 1888 the 30 year old Rudolph had an affair with 17 year old Baroness Marie Vetsera. When Emperor Franz Joseph insisted that the affair should be ended, it is said that the couple agreed to a suicide pact. According to some accounts, while staying at Rudoph's hunting lodge at Mayerling he first shot Marie and then himself. There has been much speculation over what really happened, but whatever the truth may be, Empress Elizabeth never got over her son's death and spent the rest of her life in mourning, wearing either black or pearl grey. The tragic love story has been portrayed in many films and also in ballet entitled *Mayerling*.

Sarajevo

With the death of Rudolph the line of succession went to his nephew, Archduke Franz Ferdinand who had married morganatically the Countess Sophie Chotek. Since Sophie was not fully accepted at the Viennese Court, the couple frequently visited the Eastern parts of the Empire where Sophie took her rightful place alongside her husband. They often visited the Balkans where Franz Ferdinand was aware of the need to raise the image of the monarchy among populations where there was an element of discontent and calls for independence. In this way he also satisfied his need to be doing something, rather than simply waiting in the wings for the now elderly Franz Joseph to die.

It was on one such visit, on the 28th June AD 1914, that Franz Ferdinand and his wife Sophie were shot by an anarchist in Sarajevo, which was then the Austria-Hungarian capital of Bosnia and Herzegovina. The assassin was a Bosnian Serb named Gavrilo Princip, who belonged to a party opposed to Austria-Hungarian rule.

The shooting prompted the Austrians to attack Serbia, which in turn resulted in the Russians coming in on the side of Serbia, followed by the Germans joining the Austrians; and so began the blood bath of the First World War.

The end of the First World War, in AD 1918, marked the end of Empire. The Russian Empire, the German Empire, the Ottoman Empire and the Austria-Hungarian Empires were all dissolved. The age of Empire was over. A new era had begun. It was to be an era with many new problems but the traditions of Empire, whether for good or for bad, remain in the lifeblood of central Europe.

*****

EPILOGUE

Emperor Franz Joseph died in AD 1916 at the age of 86, two years into the First World War. The children of the assassinated Franz Ferdinand were excluded from the line of succession on account of their father's morganatic marriage. The line of succession therefore went to Charles, the first son of Otto, another nephew of Franz Joseph. Although Charles was not prepared for the succession, his marriage to Zita of Bourbon-Parma, a woman of royal lineage put him in good stead. He was also an extremely devout Catholic.

Charles' rule as Emperor of the Austria-Hungarian Empire was short-lived. Following the dissolution of the Empire after the First World War, Charles and his family went into exile in Madeira. He never did officially abdicate the throne, always hoping for the restoration of the monarchy. He died in AD 1922 from pneumonia at the early age of 34. Known as the *Blessed Charles of Austria* he was beatified by the Catholic Church in AD 2004.

Otto, first son of Charles succeeded his father as Head of the House of Habsburg. Known as the Archduke of Austria, Otto was politically active throughout his life. He was a great supporter of European integration and spoke out against Nazism and communism. He died in AD 2011 in Germany at the age of 98 and is buried in the Imperial Crypt in Vienna.

Today's Head of the House of Habsburg is Karl, first son of Otto. He is also Sovereign of the Order of the Golden Fleece, an Order that was founded in AD 1430 by Philip III of Burgundy. Karl has served as a Member of the European Parliament and the Austrian People's Party. He has one son who was born in Salzburg in AD 1997. In true Habsburg fashion the child was named Ferdinand. As heir to the royal dynasty his title is Grand Duke of Austria, although all Imperial titles are now illegal in Austria and Hungary.

The Habsburg dynasty continues despite the end of Empire. From the time of Charles the Great in AD 800 until today, there has been a continual sense of Imperial duty combined with a strong commitment to uphold the faith of the Catholic Church. These have created an unbreakable thread that has lasted some fourteen hundred years.

*****

CHRONOLOGY

AD

800	Coronation of Charles the Great
843	Treaty of Verdun
962	Coronation of Otto I as Holy Roman Emperor
1122	Concordat of Worms (Investiture Controversy)
1356	Golden Bull (formalising electoral procedure)
1459	Maximilian I, Holy Roman Emperor
1517	Beginning of European Reformation
1519	Charles V, Holy Roman Emperor
1529	Siege of Vienna by the Ottomans
1683	Battle of Vienna with the Ottomans
1806	Dissolution of Holy Roman Empire
1867	Creation of Austria-Hungarian Empire
1918	Dissolution of Austria-Hungarian Empire

ABOUT THE AUTHOR

Anne has had a life-long interest in history and the religions of the world. This led to her studying both topics for her first Degree and later for her Doctorate. She spent several years living overseas and this experience added to her fascination with different peoples and cultures.

For many years she was Adviser in Inter Religious Relations with the Church of England. She was also Vice Moderator of the Dialogue Unit of the World Council of Churches in Geneva and has sat on numerous advisory bodies for Inter Religious Relations around the world.

Anne also lectures regularly on cruise ships and at academic institutions around the United Kingdom and she is an Accredited Lecturer with the National Association of Fine Arts Societies.

Many of those who have heard Anne lecture have encouraged her to write a book. This book, which is based on a series of lectures, is the result of such encouragement. It is the third in the *'In Brief' Series: Books for Busy People*. Her other books in this series are: *From the Medes to the Mullahs: a history of Iran,* and *Paul of Tarsus: a First Century* Radical. Both are available at Amazon and other outlets in both e-book and paperback.

http://www.annedavison.info

*****

Printed in Great Britain
by Amazon.co.uk, Ltd.,
Marston Gate.